I0569395

Acknowledgements

One of the most inspiring gifts we can receive is an unexpected word of encouragement. I'm especially grateful to the dear friend who once shared how much she enjoyed hearing my prayers. Her words touched my heart and lifted my spirit. Then she added something unforgettable: "I would love to have a collection of them. Put them in a book." Thank you, Kippi. Your encouragement planted the seed for this project.

Lastly, thank you to my wife. Her spiritual, thoughtful, and challenging contributions helped bring this book to completion.

I pray this book will be a blessing to many others, just as their words were a blessing to me.

Forty Days of Prayer and Reflection

Strengthening Your Bond with God

by Pastor Andre d'Arden

BIBLE SCRIPTURES

Scripture quotations are from the New King James Version®.
Copyright © 1982 by Thomas Nelson. Used by permission. All rights
reserved.

Published in the United States of America by

 **SPIRIT MEDIA**

Spirit Media Inc
https://spiritmedia.us

Spirit Media and our logos are trademarks of
Spirit Media Inc
8045 Arco Corporate Drive STE 130
Raleigh, NC 27617
1 (888) 800-3744

Religion & Spirituality | Christian Books & Bibles | Spiritual Growth

Paperback ISBN: 979-8-89307-185-6
eBook ISBN: 979-8-89307-183-2
PDF ISBN: 979-8-89307-184-9
Library of Congress Control Number: 2025915464

Praise for Forty Days of Prayer

"If you are looking for a book to help encourage your prayer life, this is the book for you! This 40 day devotional by Pastor d'Arden begins each day with a verse of Scripture, a brief devotion, a thoughtful prayer along with some questions of reflection that will inspire your overall spiritual growth and relationship with God. Oftentimes, we don't know what to pray for or how to pray, but this is why the Holy Spirit was sent, to help God's people. And, one of the ways the Lord continues to inspire the faith of others is through individuals like Pastor d'Arden who fulfilled the call to write this 40 day prayer book to uplift the body of Christ. Therefore, may anyone who reads this prayer book be blessed and experience an increase in their prayer life."

Table of Contents

Introduction

Forty Days of Prayer: Strengthening Your Bond with God

The number forty holds powerful significance in Scripture. It marks seasons of testing, transformation, and divine preparation. Moses communed with God on Mount Sinai for forty days and nights, receiving the Ten Commandments that would guide the heart of a nation:

> *"Then the Lord said to Moses, 'Write these words, for according to the tenor of these words I have made a covenant with you and with Israel.' So he was there with the Lord forty days and forty nights; he neither ate bread nor drank water. And He wrote on the tablets the words of the covenant, the Ten Commandments"* **(Exodus 34:27–28, NKJV)**

The Israelites wandered in the wilderness for forty years, being shaped as God's covenant people before entering the Promised Land. Elijah traveled forty days to Mount Horeb in search of renewed purpose.

And our Lord Jesus Christ, before stepping into His public ministry, fasted for forty days and nights in the wilderness, resisting the temptations of Satan and emerging empowered by the Spirit:

> *"Then Jesus was led up by the Spirit into the wilderness to be tempted by the devil. And when He had fasted forty days and forty nights, afterward He was hungry. Now when the tempter came to Him..."* **(Matthew 4:1–3, NKJV)**

"Immediately the Spirit drove Him into the wilderness. And He was there in the wilderness forty days, tempted by Satan, and was with the wild beasts; and the angels ministered to Him" (**Mark 1:12–13, NKJV)**

In each of these biblical accounts, the forty-day period marked a threshold between what was and what would be. It was a space where God refined, prepared, and revealed. It was a time of divine interruption—where heaven touched earth—and lives were changed forever.

In that same spirit, *Forty Days of Prayer* is an invitation to enter into your own transformative journey. These days are not meant to be rushed. They are not bound to a particular liturgical season like Lent, although they certainly echo its call to reflection, repentance, and renewal. These forty days are a sacred rhythm—a deliberate space to pause, reflect, and realign with the presence and power of God.

This devotional is not organized around a linear theme but reflects the unpredictability of life itself. The prayers, like the challenges we face, may seem random—yet God's sovereignty threads through them all. Just as the spies returned from exploring the Promised Land after forty days:

"And they returned from spying out the land after forty days."
—**Numbers 13:25, NKJV**

You too may return from this journey with a deeper sense of faith, clarity, and readiness for what God has ahead.

Your spiritual growth begins in the Scriptures—what God has said, what Jesus has taught, and what The Apostles have written. These are the foundations of our faith. As you walk through these days of prayer, may you gain a greater awareness of your need for God, develop the courage to put your ego in check, and embrace a life marked by humility, self-discipline, and trust.

Faith is the acknowledgment of our dependence on God's strength and guidance. It is a daily decision to respond to His presence and align with His purposes—even when life feels uncertain. Through these pages, you are invited to pour out your heart before the Lord, to seek His will, and to be renewed by the Spirit.

This journey is not just about getting through forty days—it's about what God does in you during them.

So take a breath.

Take the days as they come.

And walk them with God.

Let the rhythm of prayer guide you through the next forty days.

"The lamp of the body is the eye.
Therefore, when your eye is good, your
whole body also is full of light. But when
your eye is bad, your body also is full of
darkness. Therefore take heed that the
light which is in you is not darkness.
If then your whole body is full of light,
having no part dark, the whole body will
be full of light, as when the bright shining
of a lamp gives you light."
(LUKE 11:34-36, NKJV)

DAY 1
HEALING FOR WHOLENESS

Gracious Father, hear our petition submitted to your throne of grace. Hear the cries from our broken hearts. Hear our request for Wholeness: healing of mind, body, and soul. Give us happiness and joy. Allow us to have times of celebration. Help us to deal with grief and difficult situations. We ask you to shorten our cries and then add excitement to our day. Stop the tears from falling from our eyes and bring restoration and wholeness. In addition, we ask you to stop the persistent attack of cancer on our ailing bodies and give us relief from the pain.

You only hear the prayers of those who fall humbly before your throne of grace. So we sincerely present our petition and supplications to you from a sincere heart. There is no other refuge to turn to. So we turn to you, and you alone, in this time of need. We pray to the God who heals, comforts and brings Wholeness. Hear our prayer, we pray.
Amen.

Everyone desires a whole healthy mind, body and soul. But when a portion of our being is not in harmony with the whole, our life is not in balance.

How can you tell when your relationship with God and others is not in harmony or balance?

_____

_____

_____

_____

How does being out of balance affect other areas of your life?

_____

_____

_____

_____

Write a prayer addressing this issue of out of harmony and balance with God and others.

_____

_____

_____

_____

_____

_____

_____

_____

_____

_____

_____

_____

_____

_____

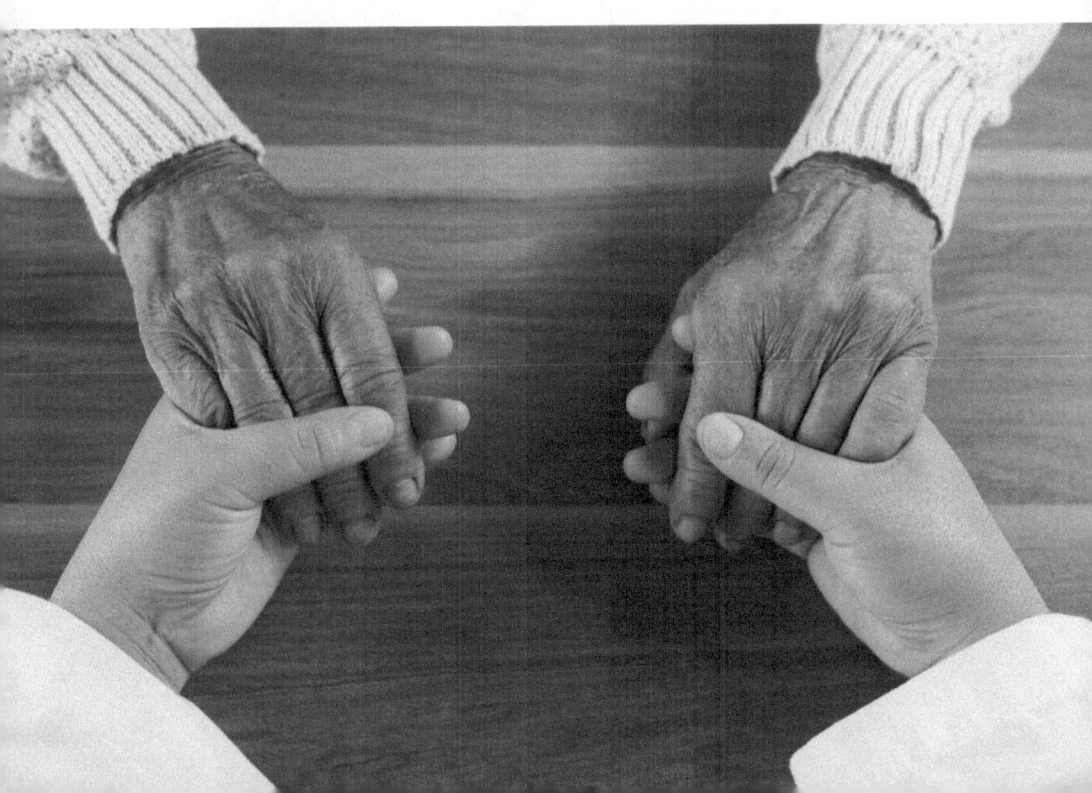

"You whom I have taken from the ends of the earth, and called from its farthest regions, and said to you, 'You are My servant, I have chosen you and have not cast you away: Fear not, for I am with you; be not dismayed, for I am your God. I will strengthen you, yes, I will help you, I will uphold you with My righteous right hand.'"

(ISAIAH 41:8-10, NKJV)

DAY 2
REMOVING THE LIMITATIONS

You, O Lord, have removed the limitations on our lives and have broken the chains that had us bound. There are no gates or walls to restrain us. We no longer have to live a sinful way of life. With no limitations we can pursue our most treasured dreams, unbounded from being obsessed with the evil of this world because we are intensely occupied with the goodness of God. We don't have to display fake love, because we are real in our hearts. The people around us benefit from our genuine love. We can move forward in life because you are on our side and nothing can hold us back.

On your behalf we will put our energy and efforts into what you desire. We expect to reach higher heights by constantly keeping our focus on you. So we ask you, grab us and hold us close in your arms. For we know, by your grace, there are no limitations to what we can do through the power you have granted us.

Our highest goals, minus our paralyzing doubts, equals powerful faith. We can hear your voice telling us; Don't lower your expectations; reach for your top performance. Because I am there with you every step of the way. To the Father, Son and Holy Spirit.
Amen, Amen, and Amen.

Surely there are some things we cannot do. But, many of us see limitations on things we really can do.

_____

_____

_____

_____

Can you see past your limitations and see the possibilities God has preserved for you?

_____

_____

_____

_____

How is your faith active in your understanding of your perceived limitations?

_____

_____

_____

_____

DAY 2: REMOVING THE LIMITATIONS

_____

_____

_____

_____

_____

_____

_____

_____

_____

_____

"All men shall fear, and shall declare the work of God; for they shall wisely consider His doing."
(PSALM 64:9, NKJV)

DAY 3

THE WORK OF GOD
IN OUR LIVES

Heavenly Father, we want to show you that your work on our behalf is sincerely appreciated. It has brought important blessings to us. It has produced a lifetime of benefits. What you have done in the past, we know you can do it again. You have shown us the best way out of difficult situations and encouraged us to keep moving straight ahead. To not pause. To not stop, but to keep on keeping on.

By being obedient to your word, we've gained courage and increased faith, and valuable experience with you. As it is written in 1 Corinthians 2:9, "But as it is written: 'Eye has not seen, nor ear heard, nor have entered into the heart of man the things which God has prepared for those who love Him.'"(NKJV) May the Grace of God, the power of the Holy Spirit rest, rule, and abide in our lives forever. Amen.

How do you see God working in your life right now?

_____

_____

_____

_____

What have your experiences with God in the past taught you?

_____

_____

_____

_____

DAY 3: THE WORK OF GOD IN OUR LIVES

_____

_____

_____

_____

_____

_____

_____

_____

_____

_____

📖

"But you be watchful in all things, endure afflictions, do the work of an evangelist, fulfill your ministry."
(2 TIMOTHY 4:5, NKJV)

DAY 4

HOLD OUT TO SEE THE WONDER OF GOD

To God the Father and Jesus Christ our Lord, When things are difficult and miserable, we only need to pray and hold out to see the mighty works of your hand. You are the one who makes us strong enough to endure. Even when the situation seems intimidating and dark, we should not give up, because we know that You are not giving up on us. We will cling to your hand until your Holy Spirit instills us with your power.

We know there are trials we must go through. But holding on to your hand leads us through perilous times. By doing so we will see the darkness turns to light and the dusk turns to dawn. Make the fog in our lives fade away and clear up. It is exciting to see your wondrous works. Giving up is not an option for us because you have shown us a victorious end to our tribulation. Thank you for the many blessings you have given us. Grace, mercy, and peace from God the Father and Jesus Christ the son ourLord. Amen.

How would you describe the experience of enduring in the midst of a trial?

_____

_____

_____

_____

How would you encourage someone to hold on until victory is achieved?

_____

_____

_____

_____

Write a prayer for someone going through hard times.

_____

_____

_____

_____

_____

_____

_____

_____

_____

_____

_____

_____

_____

"Surely goodness and mercy shall follow
me all the days of my life; and I will dwell
in the house of the Lord forever."
(PSALM 23:6 , NKJV)

DAY 5
PRAYER FOR A GOOD LIFE

Heavenly Father,

With deep thankfulness and appreciation, we are in awe of **Your** love. We recognize the wonder and miracle of life itself. Thank You for allowing us to enjoy the goodness of our existence. We cherish this gift of life, for we are alive to live another day—and another year.

A year of a good life has now passed, and it is something to be fondly remembered. Now we set the past aside and look ahead with hope for the future. For as **Your Word** says, *"Eye has not seen, nor ear heard, nor have entered into the heart of man the things which God has prepared for those who love Him"* (1 Corinthians 2:9, NKJV).

We are grateful for **Your** generosity, which has touched our everyday lives on this earth. It is **Your** will that we be as free as birds—to soar and sing our Maker's praise.

The longer we live, the more we realize how truly blessed we are. May our attitudes toward **You** reflect that growing understanding. Thank You for this good life, and forgive those who fail to appreciate its great value.

To the compassionate God we shall forever serve—

Amen.

How would you describe a blessed life to an unbeliever?

_____

_____

_____

_____

List some of the ways you can express your appreciation to God for the many blessings with which He has supplied you.

_____

_____

_____

_____

_____

_____

_____

_____

_____

_____

_____

_____

_____

_____

"Now may He who supplies seed to the sower, and bread for food, supply and multiply the seed you have sown and increase the fruits of your righteousness, while you are enriched in everything for all liberality, which causes thanksgiving through us to God. For the administration of this service not only supplies the needs of the saints, but also is abounding through many thanksgivings to God."
(2 CORINTHIANS 9:10-12, NKJV)

DAY 6

MAY WE BE FILLED
WITH ENOUGH

Lord God Jesus,

Sometimes we ask for more than what we really need. But today, we are asking You for just enough.

We are not asking for a job we are not qualified for, or to own a car we can't afford, or to win a race we have not trained for. To the God whom we call Jesus, we simply ask: Give us enough of everything that we need—so we can live our lives in the happiness of Your Spirit.

We need a way to make a living, food to eat, a safe place to live, and clothing to wear. What we don't need is an excessive amount of anything. If You choose to give us more than we ask for, we'll see it as icing on the cake.

Having enough feels like sitting in the rocking chair of Your arms. It is the destination point of our mature faith. When we have reached contentment and are satisfied, grant us a spirit of gratitude for the many blessings You have sent our way.

Give us enough hunger for Your Word, enough thirst for righteousness, and enough desire to be holy. When we have been tried and tested, and have passed the test with flying colors, we will have all that we need to be faithful.

Then we will testify: "The Lord is my shepherd; I shall not want" (Psalm 23:1, NKJV)—because You have given us enough of everything that we need.

That is why we pray to the God who is able to keep us from falling, and to present us faultless before the presence of His glory with exceeding joy.

To the only wise God our Savior, be glory and majesty, dominion and power, both now and forevermore. Amen.

One thing is for sure, God has given us enough of all that we need, and the freedom and power to pursue more time, food, gifts, strength, room, money, sleep, family, God's Holy Spirit, spiritual gifts, love, and attention. God has given us enough years to live before death.

Have you ever considered what is enough for you in all aspects of life?

_____

_____

How do you measure what is enough?

_____

_____

God has given you all the tools you need to accomplish what He wants you to do. What more would you want and why?

_____

_____

_____

_____

_____

_____

_____

_____

_____

_____

_____

_____

"I can do all things through
Christ who strengthens me."
(PHILIPIANS 4:13, NKJV)

DAY 7

WHAT CAN GOD DO THROUGH YOU

Jesus, our Redeemer,

The Devil has convinced some of us that we can't do certain things, that we can't reach the goals we have set for ourselves, and that we can't do better than what we are doing right now. But I make the announcement today: the Devil is lying.

Once the children of God believe that the Devil is a liar, they will begin to believe what the Word of God truly says—that we can do all things through Christ who strengthens us (Phil. 4:13, NKJV).

O Lord, help us to believe that Your power is unlimited and that we have access to it—that You want to use Your power through us. Help us to believe that it has no restrictions, no limits, and no end. Speak to us, Lord, so that we will know we are stronger than we believe—because You are our strength and our strong tower. Increase our faith in You and in ourselves.

Inspire us to believe. Help us to cast out all doubt. Let our imaginations run wild with belief that Your power can propel us to higher heights. We don't know our limits until we have tried to reach them through You. Help us to take our feet off the brakes of doubt so You can have Your way in our lives—so You can work through us.

Surprise us, Lord, with what You can do through us. Convince us through Your Holy Spirit power. We vow today to allow You to use us. Reveal to us that we are better than we think we are. We have more than we thought we had. We can go further than we thought we could go. We can reach higher than we thought we could reach.

We render our will to You, so that You can pull the best out of us, because: "Eye has not seen, nor ear heard, nor have entered into the heart of man the things which God has prepared for those who love Him" (1 Cor. 2:9, NKJV).

Through the mighty name of Jesus, I pray.

Amen.

People who have low self-esteem usually don't think they can accomplish much in life. In the Christian walk of life we find this to be spiritual low self-esteem.

How would you go about improving this condition?

_____

_____

_____

_____

Who can help you in this endeavor?

_____

_____

_____

_____

_____

_____

_____

_____

_____

_____

_____

_____

_____

_____

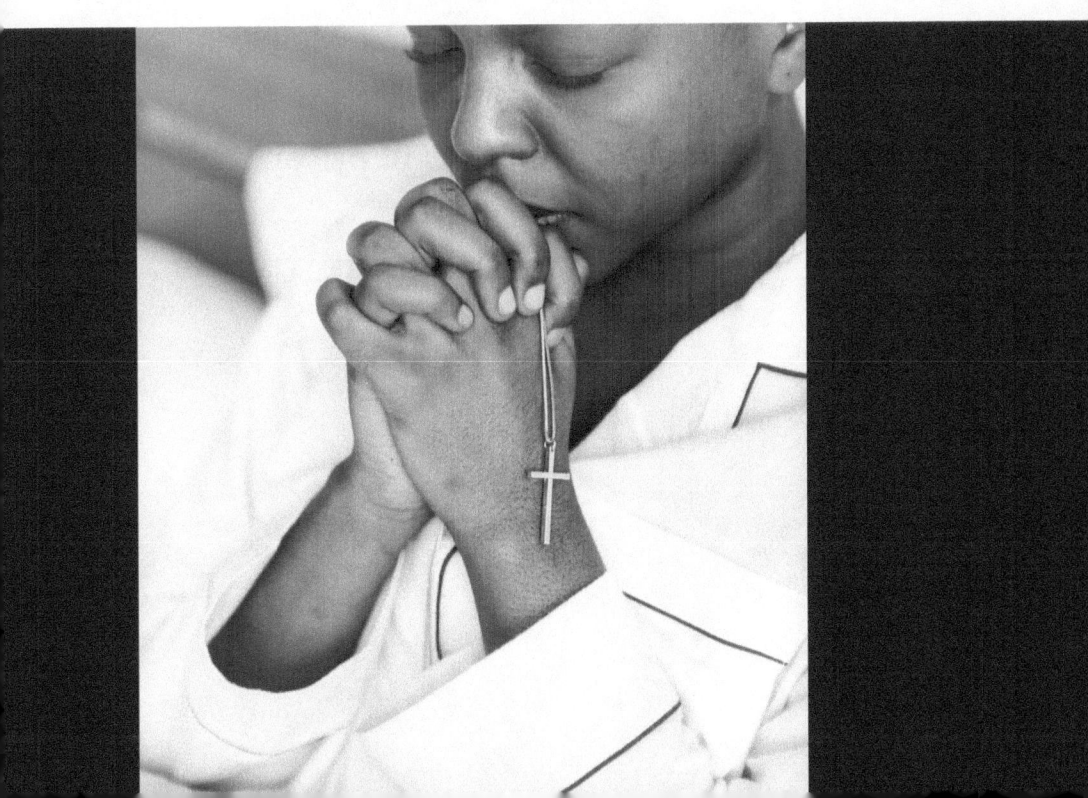

✝

"Then the King will say to those on His right hand, 'Come, you blessed of My Father, inherit the kingdom prepared for you from the foundation of the world: for I was hungry and you gave Me food; I was thirsty and you gave Me drink; I was a stranger and you took Me in; I was naked and you clothed Me; I was sick and you visited Me; I was in prison and you came to Me.'"
(MATTHEW 25:34-36, NKJV)

DAY 8

TEACH US TO SERVE YOU LORD

Teach me, O Lord, to serve You in the right way.

I want to serve You with my whole heart, mind, body, and soul. I want to learn to give You my all and all. So I ask You to take me by the hand and lead me to do those things in the right way. I want to do them *Your* way, not *my* way—not when it is convenient for me, but when it is pleasing to You. Not when it makes *me* look good, but when it brings glory to *You.*

Help me perform true service to You, like Jesus did—by humbling myself to serve others, to wash their feet, to take time to teach others Your ways, and to demonstrate how to care for one another. This is the true service to You, God, that I desire.

Inspire me, Lord, and I will be Your devoted servant, moved by the power of Your Holy Spirit.

Amen.

Jesus taught us that what we have done to the least we have done to Him. This is service at its best. Not just worshiping him. Not just singing praises to God. It is when we do acts of kindness. When we visit the sick, shut-ins, and those imprisoned. It is when we are giving words of wisdom to a lost soul, giving much needed direction to confused men or women.

On a scale of 1 to 10, how would you rate your service to God? (1 being the least and 10 being the greatest)

_____

_____

_____

_____

What is needed for you to do better?

_____

_____

_____

_____

DAY 8: TEACH US TO SERVE YOU LORD

_____

_____

_____

_____

_____

_____

_____

_____

_____

_____

"Incline your ear and hear the words
of the wise, and apply your heart to my
knowledge; for it is a pleasant thing if
you keep them within you; let them all
be fixed upon your lips, so that your trust
may be in the Lord; I have instructed you
today, even you."
(PROVERBS 22:17-19, NKJV)

DAY 9
AIM OUR FOCUS

O Lord,

Our present circumstances have taken our attention away from what is most important. Help us to refocus on You. We need to fight against the things that distract us from Your Church's mission and direct our emotions and efforts toward You.

Our hesitation to step outside of our comfort zones—and our feelings of inadequacy—distract us from giving You the time You deserve. Sometimes, we are gripped by fear and a sense of loss. Make our spirits resonate with Your Spirit, that we may shake off these distractions and be guided in the right direction. Put Your purpose back in our line of sight so we may clearly see the target we have been missing. Our bull's-eye should always be fixed on Your will.

Refresh our energy and renew our enthusiasm to do things we have never done before. Then, we will stop letting circumstances discourage us.

You are the bright light that can block out the noise of this world and push it out of our sight. Focus all of our inner strength on the mission at hand. Open our eyes so that we may see our way out of the mess we are in. Awaken our sleepy eyes so we may clearly see through these fearful times.

In the name of Jesus Christ, I pray. Amen.

Distractions interfere with all of us on one occasion or another. What distractions have been in your life?

_____

_____

_____

_____

How have you dealt with these distractions successfully?

_____

_____

_____

_____

Which ones were the most difficult and why?

_____

_____

_____

_____

_____

_____

_____

_____

_____

_____

_____

_____

_____

_____

†

"...being confident of this very thing, that He who has begun a good work in you will complete it until the day of Jesus Christ;"
(PHILIPPIANS 1:6, NKJV)

DAY 10
GOD IS NOT FINISHED WITH ME YET

Lord,

Help me to reject the false belief that miracles don't exist, that prophecies have ceased, and that I have reached my limit. I need to reject the idea that I cannot grow any further or that there is nothing more I can do for Your mission.

Help me find a way to see that You are not finished with me yet. There are many more things You are asking me to do. So I say: Use me, Lord, in Your service—in my home, on my job, wherever I am needed, and wherever I may go. Then the world will see You working in me.

You have begun a good work in me, and You will continue until I have reached higher heights and achieved a higher purpose. Work in my life until the mission is finally complete.

Whatever I may accomplish is not mine to claim—the credit belongs to You.

To God be the honor and the glory forever and ever. Amen.

All Christian believers are a work in progress. It is an admirable desire to want to reach higher, go further, and accomplish more than you have.

Is there a higher purpose that you desire to achieve?

_____

_____

_____

_____

DAY 10: GOD IS NOT FINISHED WITH ME YET

_____

_____

_____

_____

_____

_____

_____

_____

_____

_____

"Tell your children about it, Let your children tell their children, And their children another generation."
(JOEL1:3, NKJV)

DAY 11
NURTURE

To the only God who has shown concern for us,

There are people who show no concern for their children. This must change. They should not leave their children to their own devices—in a state of immaturity and lacking knowledge. A parent's responsibility is to nurture their children, so they can avoid the mistakes we, as adults, have made, and be steered away from as many pitfalls as possible.

We ask You, Lord Jesus, to come and see about Your adult children, who now need You to nourish them with Your wisdom and mature them through Your faith. Instill in them virtue.

Make our actions take root and grow, so that we can pass them on to the next generation. We look forward to seeing the fruit of the labor You have placed in us. We seek to bring out the best in our children—to give them the strength to hold on to the promises of God, to motivate and inspire them in the faith, and to create an atmosphere where they can learn to trust in You by watering the seeds of faith and fanning the sparks of spiritual curiosity within them.

By doing these things, they will rise above skepticism and doubt and come to know the benefits of living their lives in Christ Jesus. Because of You, we will be blessed with great delight and fulfillment as we witness the fruit of our labor: seeing our children grow, achieve, and overcome obstacles.

If it had not been for You, we would still be living in darkness. Thank You for the optimism of faith that leads us to hope and confidence in the gospel of Christ Jesus.

Amen.

Have you been so fortunate to have someone lovingly nurture you through life?

_____

_____

_____

_____

What part do you remember best about the process?

_____

_____

_____

_____

Did it impress upon you to do the same for someone else?

_____

_____

_____

_____

_____

_____

_____

_____

_____

_____

_____

_____

_____

_____

"That the genuineness of your faith, being much more precious than gold that perishes, though it is tested by fire, may be found to praise, honor, and glory at the revelation of Jesus Christ."
(1 Peter 1:7, NKJV)

DAY 12
AUTHENTICALLY CHRISTIAN

Holy and Righteous Lord,

We don't want to live our lives as superficial Christians, impersonating Jesus. We don't want to project the imitation of a loving person—we want to be a truly loving person. There are enough fake people in the world, and we don't want to add to their numbers. We don't want to pretend to care. We want to genuinely care. We want to live every moment of every day filled with authenticity.

Help us to be completely truthful on the inside so our integrity will shine on the outside. Sincerity in our hearts will drive us to do right and be right, causing us to live abundant and fruitful lives. Brighten the pathway before us. Help us to choose to live carefully—to be wise and not unwise. Every day, we want to strive to learn how to exhibit integrity. Fill us with an authentic spirit.

We can talk and walk like Jesus because we have the Holy Spirit residing in us. May we, as Your church, shine like a house on a hill that cannot be hidden. Let us be the light of the world that shines brilliantly, so that others may see our good works and glorify You, God.

May we be authentic followers of Christ Jesus.

In the holy name of Jesus, I pray. Amen.

The conviction in the heart of being insincere or fake can produce a heavy load of guilt.

What steps can one take to rectify this situation?

_____

_____

_____

_____

Which Scriptures are most useful to move us in the direction of becoming authentically Christian?

_____

_____

_____

_____

_____

_____

_____

_____

_____

_____

_____

_____

_____

_____

_____

"That the genuineness of your faith, being much more precious than gold that perishes, though it is tested by fire, may be found to praise, honor, and glory at the revelation of Jesus Christ."
(1 Peter 1:7, NKJV)

DAY 13

CONSTANT SPIRITUAL PROGRESS

Heavenly Father,

Too often we see the bad in the world more than the good. We need You to help us prevent the bad news of life from discouraging us and dampening our spirits. We need constant spiritual progress. Reveal the best in life to us so that we can see Your wonderful work. Don't allow the darkness in the world to discourage us. Put Your words of wisdom in our mouths, that we may grow in wisdom and increase understanding in our hearts. Help us always to carry a positive attitude and produce actions that bear fruit of faith.

Therefore, we beseech You to knock on the door of our hearts forever. In doing so, we will be able to pledge an unwavering commitment to Your Word. Our hope is to forever embrace the transformative journey of constant spiritual progress. It will rewrite the story of our lives.

Today, we hang our trust on Your every word. We reach for Your high standards, and we will keep opening new doors and doing good things on Your behalf. Now and forever, we will be the best people we can be—thanks to the only wise God, our Savior.

Amen.

Tracking one's spiritual progress is probably a foreign idea that does not resonate with the average worshipper.

How can you institute spiritual progress?

_____

_____

_____

_____

How would you track your spiritual progress?

_____

_____

_____

_____

_____

_____

_____

_____

_____

_____

_____

_____

_____

_____

_____

"That you may walk worthy of the Lord, fully pleasing Him, being fruitful in every good work and increasing in the knowledge of God; strengthened with all might, according to His glorious power, for all patience and longsuffering with joy."
(Colossians 1:10-11, NKJV)

DAY 14

THE HANDS OF GOD

Our Everlasting God,

All day long You have held out Your mighty hands to disobedient and contrary people. You continuously toil in the vineyard with us. You jump right into the thick of things to give us Your helping hand. We are assured Your hands will never leave us alone. You are the lifter of our souls—the protector of our lives. Your hands are firm in guiding us in the right direction.

How sad it would be if we did not give our hands to help in Your mission. Your hands will catch us to break the fall. Help us to see Your hand extended to pull us away from the brink of disaster and shield us from flying stones.

Now is the time for us to make things right before Your throne of grace. We humble ourselves under Your mighty hand, that You may exalt us in due time. We cast all our cares on You, for You care for us. Your hand is the hand we will gladly hold on to. We trust that our lives are in Your hands.

You never grow weary and have never let us down. Your hands will be our secure place forever. Thank You for Your overwhelming love—we can't imagine how You could love us any better.

Hallelujah to God Almighty. Amen.

In what circumstance did you feel the need to ask God to help you?

_____

_____

_____

_____

What made you aware that God was reaching out to support you?

_____

_____

_____

_____

_____

_____

_____

_____

_____

_____

_____

_____

_____

_____

†

"And I said to them, 'You are holy to the Lord; the articles are holy also; and the silver and the gold are a freewill offering to the Lord God of your fathers.'"
(Ezra 8:28, NKJV)

DAY 15

GOD'S GIFT OF LIFE IS WORTH IT

With this life that You created for us, O Lord, comes joy and grief, pain and pleasure, sadness and happiness, problems and great wonders. Nevertheless, life is worth all the troubles—especially when we think of the alternative. Lord, You told us to be of good cheer because You have overcome the world. So today, even in the midst of trials, we choose to cling to that victory.

You never promised that the road would be easy—but You did promise that we would never walk it alone. When the weight feels too heavy, remind us that *"My strength is made perfect in weakness"* (2 Corinthians 12:9, NKJV). When fear tries to take root, let us hear Your words again: *"Fear not, for I am with you"* (Isaiah 41:10, NKJV). Help us to rejoice—not in the hardship itself, but in what You are producing through it. Because Your Word says that *"the testing of your faith produces patience"* (James 1:3, NKJV), and that patience will make us *"perfect and complete, lacking nothing"* (James 1:4, NKJV).

We thank You for the peace that only You can give—a peace that surpasses understanding and calms every storm. Lord, give us endurance when we are weary, faith when we feel like giving up, and joy even in sorrow—because we know that You are working all things together for our good.

You have overcome, and because of that, we can stand firm in hope. Life's many troubles will come and go, but Your power will remain forever. Your blessings are our good fortune. We are grateful for the opportunity to reaffirm and recommit our faith in You. For the rest of our lives, we will call on the Lord, because *"The Lord also will be a refuge for the oppressed, a refuge in times of trouble"* (Psalm 9:9, NKJV).

Blessed be our Savior and Victor, Jesus Christ our Lord. Amen.

Imagine taking all of the negativism out of life. What would remain? Even though we can't do that, it is amazing that there can still be joy even in the midst of it all.

How can you encourage someone to value life deeply, regardless of the occasional disasters that come our way?

_____

_____

_____

_____

_____

_____

_____

_____

_____

_____

"But may the God of all grace, who called us to His eternal glory by Christ Jesus, after you have suffered a while, perfect, establish, strengthen, and settle you."
(1 PETER 5:10, NKJV)

DAY 16
PRAYER FOR REASSURANCE

Reassure us, O Lord, that when we are frightened, there will be a brighter day ahead. Reassure us that You are here with us—to give us strength to endure whatever comes our way. Reassure us that the only need we have in this world is the need for You to be by our side—to hold us in Your loving arms, give us comfort, and increase our faith.

When we begin to lose faith, restore our confidence in Your power and Your promise. Forgive us when we are stressed over nothing, when we worry unnecessarily, and when we complain. We know that You are able to release us from anxiety and distress.

We won't have a wishy-washy attitude about what we believe in. We will stand firm to proclaim the gospel of Jesus Christ. Allow the presence of Your Holy Spirit to dwell in our worship in a powerful way.

In the name of Jesus, I pray. Amen.

Are you experiencing a time of suffering?

_____

_____

_____

_____

What do you think God is establishing and strengthening in you through it?

_____

_____

_____

_____

_____

_____

_____

_____

_____

_____

_____

_____

_____

_____

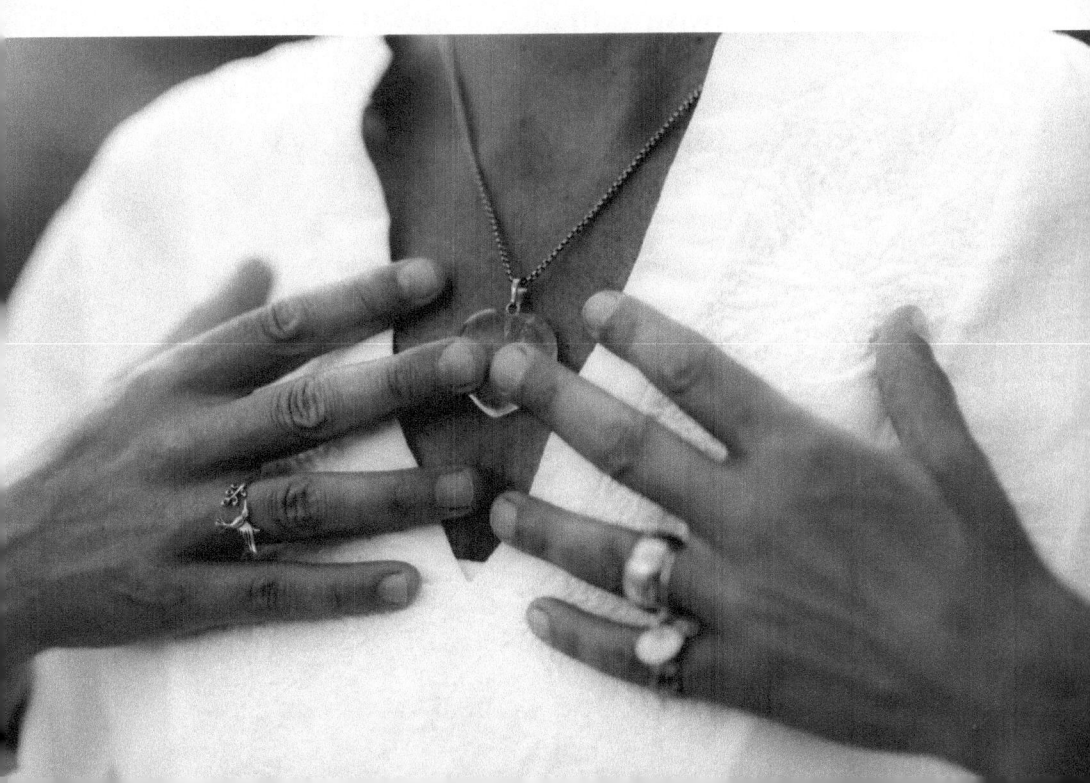

📖

"No temptation has overtaken you except as is common to man; but God is faithful, who will not allow you to be tempted beyond what you are able, but with the temptation will also make the way of escape, that you may be able to bear it."
(1 CORINTHIANS 10:13, NKJV)

DAY 17

LIFE IS NOT A BED OF ROSES

O Lord,

In the beginning, You set up life to be a beautiful bed of roses. But after the fall of Adam, it became like a bed of thorns. We should not think that we are so privileged that we should not experience heartaches and sadness in this life, or that we should be exempt from the pain of failure and disappointment.

We should not believe that only happiness, success, and joy should come our way. Our true privilege is having You constantly with us—to see us through the journey of life. Life is not a bed of roses; it is a mixture of happiness and pain, excitement and disappointment. Thank You for helping us through all of it.

When we fail and fall down, You are there to pick us up and give us strength to carry on. When we experience disasters in our lives, we should not ask the question, "Why me, Lord?" But when we experience great blessings and good fortune, we should ask, "Why me, Lord?"

Those who are spiritually mature understand that the rain falls on the good and the bad. There is great joy in knowing that You are there for us all the time.

We ask You to instill understanding in our hearts and minds as we attempt to live according to Your will. Help us keep the perspective that this world is not our home—for You have prepared a better place for us in Your presence.

To You, O Lord, be all glory and majesty.
Amen, Amen, and Amen.

In the beginning of a trial or tribulation in your life, how are you able to look past the present pain to have hope for a blessed outcome?

_____

_____

_____

_____

How did you express the joy of escaping an adverse situation?

_____

_____

_____

_____

_____

_____

_____

_____

_____

_____

_____

_____

_____

_____

"For whatever is born of God overcomes the world. And this is the victory that has overcome the world—our faith."
(1 JOHN 5:4, NKJV)

DAY 18
OVERCOMER

Lord God,

Help me live a life that exemplifies faith in You. If I have a car accident, don't let me yield to out-of-control anger, but help me rise up and be thankful I didn't lose a limb or my life.

When I catch a cold, help me be grateful that it's not pneumonia. If my project is delayed, give me insight to see that at least it was not canceled. I want to be thankful.

Teach me to be an overcomer, so I can smile in spite of my situation. I know I cannot direct the wind, but I desire to adjust my sails and bring about a change.

Help me to use my faith to make good things happen and to successfully achieve something meaningful. I want to look beyond my present circumstances and experience hope for a better day.

I give praise and honor to You, my Almighty God.

Amen, Amen, and Amen.

Why is it difficult to be positive in negative situations?

_____

_____

_____

_____

"You are of God, little children, and have overcome them, because He who is in you is greater than he who is in the world" (1 John 4:4, NKJV) When you read this Scripture what does it tell you about yourself?

_____

_____

_____

_____

_____

_____

_____

_____

_____

_____

_____

_____

_____

_____

"...but if I am delayed, I write so that you may know how you ought to conduct yourself in the house of God, which is the church of the living God, the pillar and ground of the truth."
(1 TIMOTHY 3:15, NKJV)

DAY 19

THE TRUE FAMILY OF GOD

Heavenly Father,

We are so happy to worship You. This is a joyous occasion, and we adore it greatly. Our time away from one another has not lessened our love, nor has it weakened our faith in You. But we pray that You open our eyes to the things we have neglected and restore them to the place where they belong—in our hearts.

We pray that You strengthen the ties between us and create a renewed appreciation for our fellowship—one that should matter more than passing in the night. Help us nurture a real sense of community and friendship. Show us how to capitalize on our shared experiences. Show us how to break out of superficial Christianity and connect with each other in ways that support, build, and bolster faith.

Speak to us like You never have before. Recharge us and energize our spirits to work harder than we ever have to be true to our calling.

With Your help, we will still believe in Your saving grace, still believe in Your forgiving love, and still believe in the power of Your Holy Spirit to teach and guide us to build a genuine family of God.

This I pray in Jesus' name. Amen, Amen, and Amen.

How would you describe the loss of the family spirit in a church?

_____

_____

_____

_____

What role can you play in doing something about it?

_____

_____

_____

_____

What would you say in an appeal to God in this effort?

_____

_____

_____

_____

_____

_____

_____

_____

_____

_____

_____

_____

_____

_____

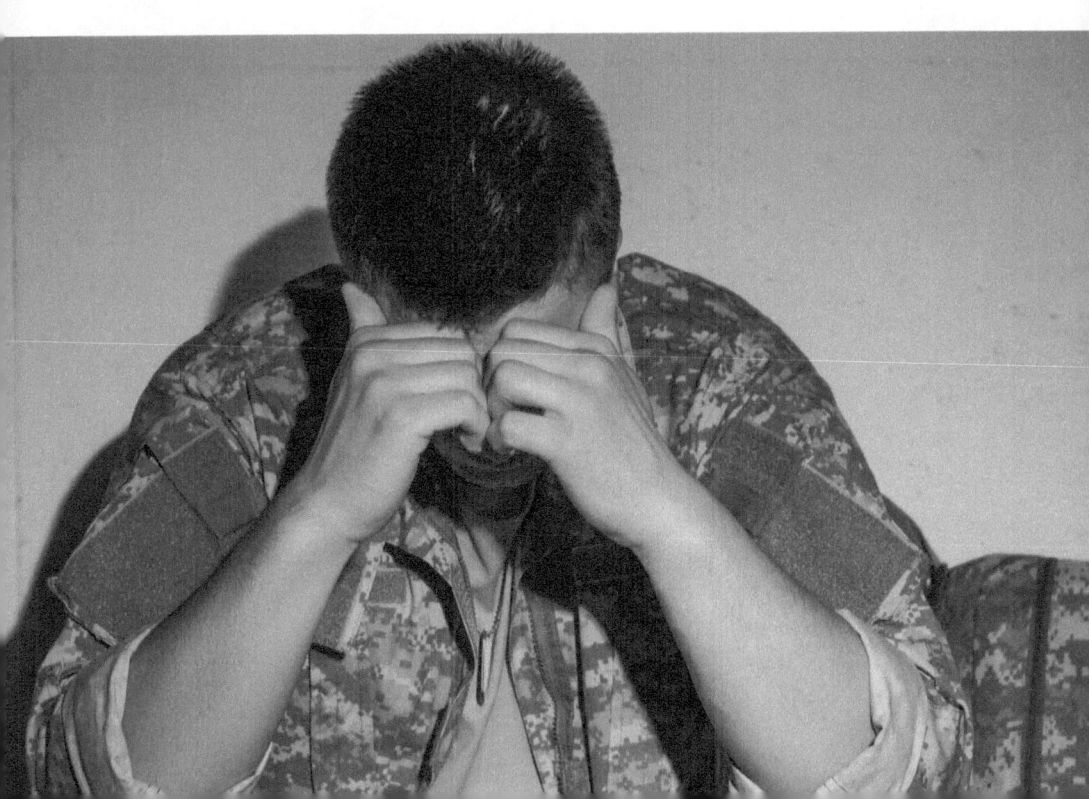

"So then, my beloved brethren, let every man be swift to hear, slow to speak, slow to wrath; for the wrath of man does not produce the righteousness of God."
(JAMES 1:19–20, NKJV)

DAY 20
CONQUERING FRUSTRATION

Precious Lord,

Disappointments discourage us and cause us to give up trying. It feels like a spinning wheel—going nowhere. We become afraid of failure and fearful of setbacks, which causes us to hesitate, if not outright give up and quit.

Give us power over these frustrations. We need to be quickened by Your Holy Spirit to strengthen us. You've done it before, and we ask You to do it again.

Make our efforts going forward unstoppable. Activate our imagination to find a way through the disappointment. With You on our side, we will not be stopped by discouragement or succumb to depression. We will fight on.

All of our fears and frustrations will be defeated. We will be invigorated and emboldened to fight the battle even harder. Expectancy will stomp out sadness. Fear will no longer betray our hearts, because You have broken the chains that once bound us.

We sincerely pray for Your intervention—with anticipation—that we may conquer disappointment with gladness.

In the name of our Almighty God, we pray. Amen.

Which Scripture helps you with disappointments and how have you overcome them?

_____

_____

_____

_____

Write something to God concerning this matter.

_____

_____

_____

_____

DAY 20: CONQUERING FRUSTRATION

_____

_____

_____

_____

_____

_____

_____

_____

_____

_____

"O house of Israel, can I not do with you
as this potter?" says the Lord. "Look, as the
clay is in the potter's hand, so are you in
My hand, O house of Israel!"
(JEREMIAH 18:6, NKJV)

DAY 21
A WORTHY VESSEL

Lord God Almighty,

We know that You desire a vessel that You can use. Not one made of iron or steel, striving to be indestructible. Not one claiming great value or adorned with costly jewelry. You desire a vessel made of clay—a vessel that is fragile and pliable, so it can be molded and fashioned to please You and reflect the character of Jesus Christ.

Not one so attractive that it competes with the beauty of God, nor one whose sparkle draws attention away from the grace of God—but one made only to be used for Your purposes.

Help us render ourselves into the type of vessel that is pleasing to You—one worthy of being used by You.

You are molding us and making us according to Your will. So we pray: transform us to bear the character of Your only begotten Son, Christ Jesus our Lord.

Amen.

How do you see yourself in service to the Lord?

_____

_____

_____

_____

If a person sought your advice and counsel by saying, "I feel the Lord has something He wants me to do, but I don't know what that is." How would you help them?

_____

_____

_____

_____

_____

_____

_____

_____

_____

_____

_____

_____

_____

_____

_____

"Then they brought little children to Him, that He might touch them; but the disciples rebuked those who brought them. But when Jesus saw it, He was greatly displeased and said to them, 'Let the little children come to Me, and do not forbid them; for of such is the kingdom of God.'"
(MARK 10:13-14, NKJV)

DAY 22
OVERCOME THE OBSTACLES

O Mighty God,

We put aside all the things that hinder us, and we join together in worship to praise Your name. We are reminded that we worship the God who created this world—the God who spoke through His prophets from generation to generation, healed the sick, fed the hungry, and remained faithful even when faced with rejection and death.

We realize that You want us to be drawn to Your love and grace, to know Your forgiveness, and to experience the joy of Your salvation. Help us to remove every obstacle so that we may have a clear path to Your outstretched arms.

Thank You for all You have done for us—the many ways You have guided us and the countless times You have shown Your love.

Gratefulness shall dwell in our hearts forever and ever.

Glory be to the Father, the Son, and the Holy Spirit. Amen.

There are a multitude of things that can hinder us from being drawn to Jesus. List a few that got in your way.

_____

_____

_____

_____

How would you explain to someone how you were able to overcome them and move them out of your way?

_____

_____

_____

_____

After they were no longer a hindrance to you, what change came over your life?

_____

_____

_____

_____

DAY 22: OVERCOME THE OBSTACLES

_____

_____

_____

_____

_____

_____

_____

_____

_____

_____

_____

"In the beginning was the Word, and the Word was with God, and the Word was God. He was in the beginning with God. All things were made through Him, and without Him nothing was made that was made. In Him was life, and the life was the light of men. And the light shines in the darkness, and the darkness did not comprehend it."
(JOHN 1:1-5, NKJV)

DAY 23

THE OWNER OF EXISTENCE

Creatures and creations belong to You. To You—and You alone—we bow and give all praise.

Belief in You can prevent the chaos people are committing and save all of humanity from the wrongs they are doing. Nowhere in the universe can we go where we will not find You there. Without You, the things You have created—and the creatures in them—cannot exist.

Thank You for the privilege of living. Life is a gift to Your beloved children. If You were to step back even a little, all of creation would decay and die. We cannot live without You.

You were here from the beginning, sustaining generations of people. And You will forever be alive—after many more generations have come and gone.

Show us how to enjoy Your presence and Your abundant blessings.

When you consider that God created the known universe and everything beyond the known and unknown galaxies, what kind of reverence, respect and honor toward God is stirred up in you?

_____

_____

_____

_____

What kind of reverence, respect and honor would you express toward Jesus?

_____

_____

_____

_____

_____

_____

_____

_____

_____

_____

_____

_____

_____

"Now thanks be to God who always leads us in triumph in Christ, and through us diffuses the fragrance of His knowledge in every place. For we are to God the fragrance of Christ among those who are being saved and among those who are perishing."
(2 CORINTHIANS 14:15, NKJV)

DAY 24
SMELL THE ROSES

Most gracious God,

As we struggle through life's experiences, we may find ourselves complaining too much. This puts roadblocks in front of us and numbs our sensitivity and awareness of how good life has been. Excessive busyness distracts us from seeing You. Teach us how to stop and smell the roses. We can miss Your marvelous works passing before us. We can fail to notice the beautiful scenery crying out for our attention.

We need to pause from our busy schedules and become aware of Your glory. Let Your words vibrate in our spirit to wake us up to all the wonderful things You have given us. Remind us that the joy You provide is better than anything the world could ever offer.

Quiet our minds, focus our attention, and touch our inward parts like none other can. Awaken us and open pathways to Your heart. Then we will see all the blessings from heaven right before our very eyes.

We need to make a point to pause, breathe, and enjoy Your creation and all the blessings in our lives. When we do, not only are our personal lives affected positively, but the force of Your Holy Spirit will ripple out into the world, impacting the lives of others.

Thanks be to God, who in Christ through us spreads the fragrance of the knowledge of God everywhere. *For we are to God the fragrance of Christ among those who are being saved* (2 Cor. 2:14–15, NKJV).

Thank You for the many blessings from on high. Amen.

How can you be the aroma of Christ in your circles of influence or even to a stranger?

_____

_____

_____

_____

Sunrise and sunset are incredible examples of God's glory in the heavens. What other examples can you come up with?

_____

_____

_____

_____

_____

_____

_____

_____

_____

_____

_____

_____

_____

_____

✝

"When I consider Your heavens, the work of Your fingers, the moon and the stars, which You have ordained, what is man that You are mindful of him, and the son of man that You visit him?"
(PSALM 8:3-4, NKJV)

DAY 25
FEELING INSIGNIFICANT

Lord God, in a universe that seems so immense, it is easy to feel insignificant. Yet as we stand here today, we know that we are precious in Your sight—unique individuals, loved and blessed in so many ways.

We stand in awe of the One who loves us just as we are. For Your glory, we were created in Your image: to shine in the world, to reflect Your love and character.

Praise we give to Your name forever. Amen.

How would you characterize how important God's children are to him?

_____

_____

_____

_____

Express to God how you feel about the depth of His love for you.

_____

_____

_____

_____

_____

_____

_____

_____

_____

_____

_____

_____

_____

_____

"And when He had removed him, He raised up for them David as king, to whom also He gave testimony and said, 'I have found David the son of Jesse, a man after My own heart, who will do all My will.'" (ACTS 13:22, NKJV)

DAY 26
WITHOUT RESERVATIONS

Our God, our King, and our Savior, we trust in Your leadership without reservation. We gladly take an oath without deliberation because Your reputation is well known to us. We have no assumptions about Your worthiness of our devotion toward You. Your Word is better than gold, and there is nothing that we can compare to it.

Even though You have given us the free will to love You or not—to obey You or not—we freely yield ourselves over to You without reservation. Our loyalty to You is more solid than an addiction. It is with delight that we give You our loyalty and dedication.

Without doubting, we choose to believe the bold claim that Jesus made: *"I am the way, the truth, and the life"* (John 14:6, NKJV). We have read His words and applied them to our lives. Now we can testify—without any reservation—that they are true.

There are millions of lives that have been changed because of them. Millions of souls have been saved by them. Countless testimonies stand as proof of Your power. They cannot be discounted. We have tried them and have found them to be reliable and trustworthy. They have set us on a firm foundation.

We will drop everything for the glory of Christ Jesus. It excites us to look forward to Your redemption and salvation.

Forever we shall praise Your name—without reservation.

Amen.

As human beings we do not and cannot know everything about God. What issues or events in the Bible have left you confused?

_____

_____

_____

_____

Pray to God, appealing for understanding and insight for that which has confounded you.

_____

_____

_____

_____

_____

_____

_____

_____

_____

_____

_____

_____

_____

_____

"For God has not given us a spirit of
fear, but of power and of love and
of a sound mind."
(2 TIMOTHY 1:7, NKJV)

DAY 27

RESISTANCE TO THE EFFECT OF FEAR

To the God of grace and power, we ask You to give us grace and empower us to live successful lives. All of the things happening around the world cause us to live our lives—not in fear—but in faith. We can only put our trust in You.

We are not asking You to allow us to walk on serpents or coals of fire without harm—not even that. We are simply asking to live our lives in peace, without fear. We resist the enemy's attempt to strike fear in our hearts. Thank You, Lord, for giving us the power to fight back because You are on our side.

We pray to be empowered so that we would not walk these streets as foolish people, but as wise believers. We cannot allow the ills of this world to stop us from receiving the blessings You have in store for us.

Fill us with Your Holy Spirit power so the enemy cannot stop us from succeeding in our business ventures and educational pursuits, nor from keeping our families safe and secure.

Lord Jesus Christ, may Your Spirit and grace be with us always. Amen. Amen.

Fear can positively or negatively affect the mind, body, and relationships.

How has fear played a role in your spiritual life?

_____

_____

_____

_____

What are the tools you need to overcome your fear?

_____

_____

_____

_____

Ask God to help you overcome fear using the tools He revealed to you.

_____

_____

_____

_____

DAY 27: RESISTANCE TO THE EFFECT OF FEAR

"Come to Me, all you who labor and are heavy laden, and I will give you rest. Take My yoke upon you and learn from Me, for I am gentle and lowly in heart, and you will find rest for your souls. For My yoke is easy and My burden is light."
(MATTHEW 11:28-30, NKJV)

DAY 28
VICTORY OVER BURDENS

We give thanks to You, our God. You have made us grateful that You are in our lives—especially when heavy burdens weigh on our minds and sadness overruns our happiness. We know that You know our burdens, You see our tears, You feel our broken hearts, and You understand our pain.

After we have dug deep inside our souls and cried out to You—then, and only then—will we know that You have heard our prayers.

We shall lift our hands to heaven, asking for deliverance, and appeal to You: make us grow strong and tall. You are the lifeguard of our faith. We ask You to stop the evil thoughts that try to make us believe our pain will never go away.

With Your help, we will keep pushing forward—even if we must crawl until we walk, and walk until we can run. Show us compassion, mercy, and grace until we find relief, joy, comfort, and fulfillment.

Help us defeat our burdens, reminding us that You have promised us abundant life. Because of You, we are breaking through the heavy burdens. And we are breaking free from the chains that have bound us. That is why we stand faithful to our promise to You.

Now, speak Your Word to our hearts, minds, bodies, and souls—so that we will not quit the battle in which we are engaged. We want to remain pleasing in Your sight, Holy God our Savior.

Amen.

What types of burdens have you had to bear?

_____

_____

_____

_____

What particular tools or skills would you ask God to give you to help a person who has been burdened for a long time?

_____

_____

_____

_____

DAY 28: VICTORY OVER BURDENS

_____

_____

_____

_____

_____

_____

_____

_____

_____

_____

"Indeed the hour is coming, yes, has now come, that you will be scattered, each to his own, and will leave Me alone. And yet I am not alone, because the Father is with Me. These things I have spoken to you, that in Me you may have peace. In the world you will have tribulation; but be of good cheer, I have overcome the world."
(JOHN 16:32-33, NKJV)

DAY 29
PULL US THROUGH

To the God who is deeply concerned about our welfare:

We know that life's difficulties are common to us all—and that none of us are alone in these experiences. The problem is, sometimes they make us feel like giving up. These are the moments when we need encouragement to keep holding on—so we won't quit fighting back, and we won't give up hope.

In moments like these, encouragement from You is what we need. You know how to speak directly to our situation, to remind us that even in the darkest moments, You are there to pull us through.

You can give us resilience and persistence to endure these struggling times. No matter how tough our challenges are, You are closer to us than we realize—ready to help us make it through. The only thing we need to do is ask You to empower us to be overcomers of problems and victors in tough times, knowing that Christ's victory on the cross overshadows all our troubles.

Life is a lot of work. But You can give us the strength to continue when we are tired and burned out. You inspire us and renew our strength to break through seemingly impossible odds.

Thank You, Lord, for being there for us—teaching us to reach out to You daily, and to take heart because You will carry us through. Infuse us with determination.

This I pray in Jesus' name. Amen.

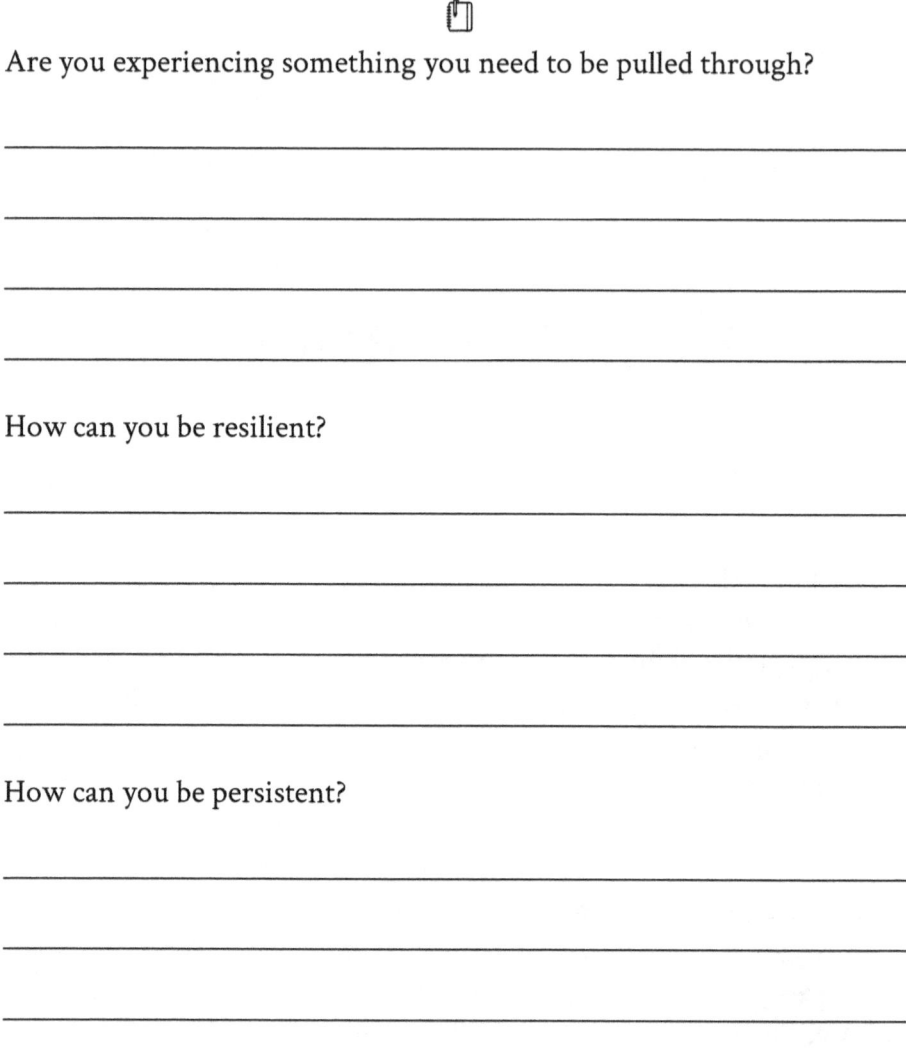

Are you experiencing something you need to be pulled through?

_____

_____

_____

_____

How can you be resilient?

_____

_____

_____

_____

How can you be persistent?

_____

_____

_____

_____

_____

_____

_____

_____

_____

_____

_____

_____

_____

"He shall pray to God, and He will delight in him, He shall see His face with joy, for He restores to man His righteousness."
(JOB 33:25-26, NKJV)

DAY 30
PRAYER FOR RECOVERY

O Lord, if any one of us ever goes through the experience of a house fire, natural disaster, addiction, or depression, help us to rely on You to guide us through recovery. Times like these can turn us into a complete wreck—but there is hope in You, Christ Jesus. You will lead us through such troubled times. You made recovery possible. It's a struggle, but You have set the way for us to rise from the ashes.

What a blessing it is to experience recovery and restoration. With You on our side, we will not be held down by hopelessness, guilt, or shame, because we will hold on to the powerful hand of Almighty God. Our eyes will see little steps of improvement—one day at a time—all the way through the process to the finish line.

In recovery, we have found our way back. We have gained a new perspective on what the power of God can do. Even though we have lost some things, through the help of the Lord we have recovered a portion of them and received new things.

Now we have a new perspective on life, because our faith is in You, our God.

In Jesus' name I pray. Amen.

What is a dire situation you are facing?

_____

_____

_____

_____

Which biblical principle can you rely on right now?

_____

_____

_____

_____

Ask the Lord to give you assistance and guidance in this situation.

_____

_____

_____

_____

_____

_____

_____

_____

_____

_____

_____

_____

_____

_____

_____

_____

"He also brought me up out of a horrible pit, out of the miry clay, and set my feet upon a rock, and established my steps."
(PSALM 40:2, NKJV)

DAY 31
LET JESUS LEAD YOU THROUGH

O Lord, we call on You to rescue those who have lost their rudder in life and feel adrift. Their situation weighs heavily on our hearts. They are moving aimlessly, blinded by the darkness of this world. Cast out their fear, and help them to know that You are there—ready to lead them.

We proclaim to the people: Trust in the Lord, and He will lead you in the right direction. You have said that You will lead us out of darkness into Your marvelous light.

We say to Your people, "Let Him carry you through the miry clay. Hear the guidance of the Lord, and He will lead you to peace and assurance."

We are asking You, Lord, and we will follow. Thank You, Jesus, that You have already established a place for us. The destination is clear. The road may be bumpy, but You can make it smooth enough so we won't stumble or fall. Help us to simply allow You to lead us.

In the name of Jesus, I pray. Amen.

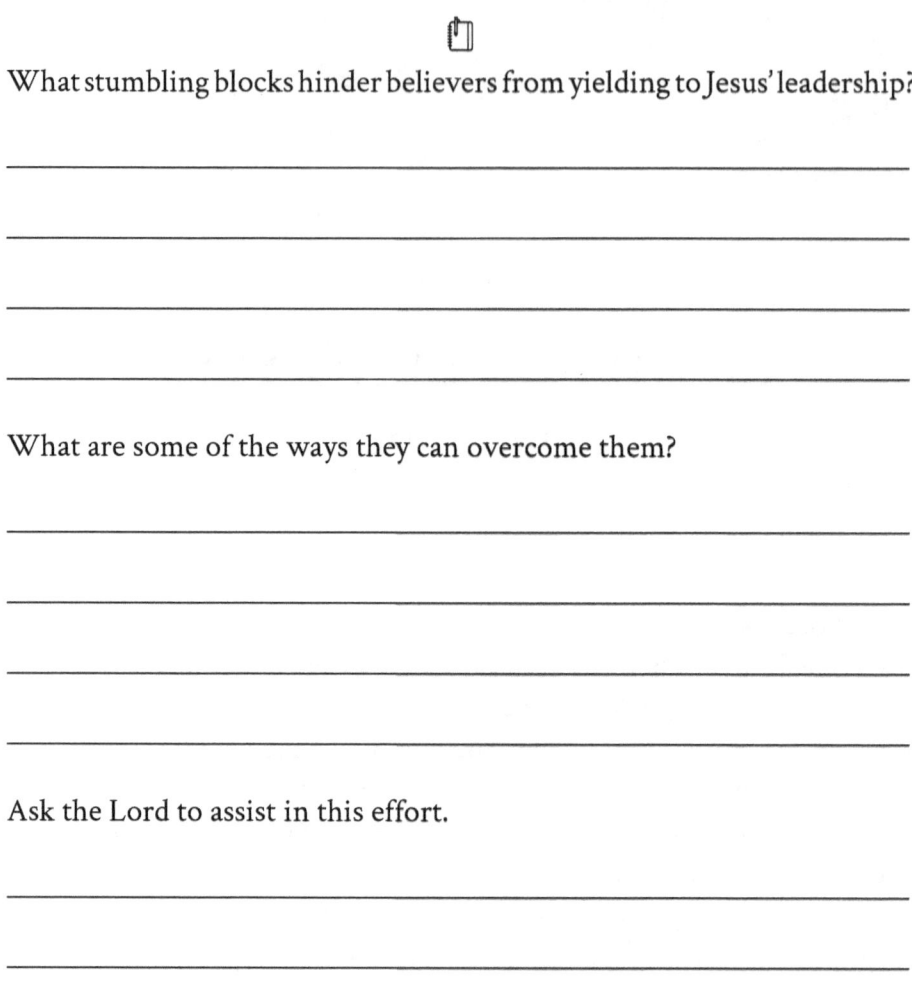

What stumbling blocks hinder believers from yielding to Jesus' leadership?

_____

_____

_____

_____

What are some of the ways they can overcome them?

_____

_____

_____

_____

Ask the Lord to assist in this effort.

_____

_____

_____

_____

_____

_____

_____

_____

_____

_____

_____

_____

_____

_____

_____

†

"Therefore, as we have opportunity, let us
do good to all, especially to those who are
of the household of faith."
(GALATIANS 6:10, NKJV)

DAY 32
MISSED OPPORTUNITIES

Oh mighty God, it would be a horrible regret to miss out on opportunities to make a positive change. Opportunities are always available. Hesitation is the enemy of missed opportunities. Shame is the punishment for action not taken. Make us aware of the many opportunities right before us. We want to experience joy for successfully following the dictates of your heart.

Send Your Holy Spirit to inspire us to get up, get going, and get-on with changing the world. You are by our side to help us find a way, to make it happen. It is not a mountain we are trying to move, but it is ourselves. We fight against lack of faith and procrastination. It will be pleasing to you, not by the big things we try to achieve, but things we are successful in achieving.

We don't want to miss out on opportunities to make a positive change. So we commit to you that we will stop wasting our time, energy and resources into doing nothing. But we shall pour out our hearts in making a real difference in someone's life. We have chosen to make a change in this world to help someone, save a soul from destruction, to ease someone's pain and comfort the comfortless. We know, You will compare our achievements to the efforts of our hearts. Your blessings are on our side. To the Almighty God our Savior, Amen.

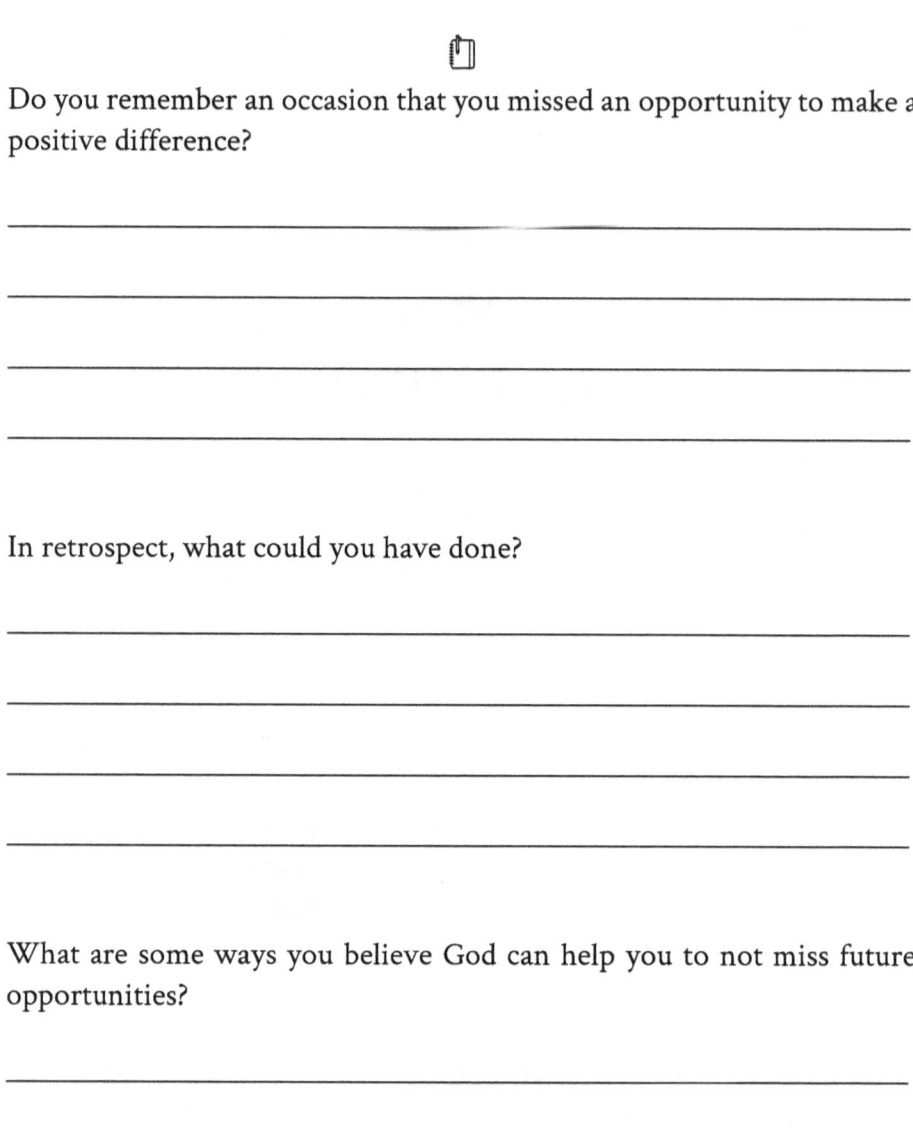

Do you remember an occasion that you missed an opportunity to make a positive difference?

_____

_____

_____

_____

In retrospect, what could you have done?

_____

_____

_____

_____

What are some ways you believe God can help you to not miss future opportunities?

_____

_____

_____

_____

Write an appeal to God.

_____

_____

_____

_____

_____

_____

_____

_____

_____

"...those who hope in the LORD will renew their strength. They will soar on wings like eagles; they will run and not grow weary, they will walk and not be faint." (ISAIAH 40:31, NKJV)

DAY 33

RESTING IN THE ARMS OF JESUS

Loving God, I pray that we, Your people, will never be like the Israelites who wandered in the wilderness—constantly grumbling and dissatisfied. It is in our best interest to learn how to trust in Your every word, to rest our hope on Your promises, and to keep any negative attitude in check before it overtakes us and causes us to fall.

Our desire is to draw closer to Your presence, rest in Your loving arms, and love You more dearly. All we need to do is follow the Scripture that says:

"But those who wait on the Lord shall renew their strength;
They shall mount up with wings like eagles,
They shall run and not be weary,
They shall walk and not faint" (Isa. 40:31, NKJV).

By placing our hope in You, our souls will be rejuvenated and strengthened.

We will gain the ability to rise above challenges, endure without weariness, and walk through life with unwavering faith. Thank You for the power of the Holy Spirit that resides in us.

This I pray in Jesus' name. Amen.

List a few lessons we can learn from Israel's failures of the past to help us in today's society.

_____

_____

_____

_____

After failing God, what are some of the ways believers can regain the favor of God?

_____

_____

_____

_____

Write a few sentences appealing to God for restoration from spiritual failure.

_____

_____

_____

_____

DAY 33: RESTING IN THE ARMS OF JESUS

_____

_____

_____

_____

_____

_____

_____

_____

_____

_____

✝

"Therefore, my beloved brethren, be steadfast, immovable, always abounding in the work of the Lord, knowing that your labor is not in vain in the Lord."
(1 CORINTHIANS 15:58, NKJV)

DAY 34
MAKE US USEFUL

Heavenly Father, while we are spending time on this earth, make us useful. Help us to inspire someone to live according to Your will. Show us the way to someone's heart. Give us new ideas and new ways to make a difference in our community.

Lead us to a lost soul, and direct us in how to guide them to salvation. Teach us how to correct the errors of our ways, so that we can be an example for others instead of a stumbling block.

We are not asking that the work we do—or the good we bring into the world—be recognized or praised by men. We do it only to please You, the God of heaven.

This I pray in Jesus' name. Amen.

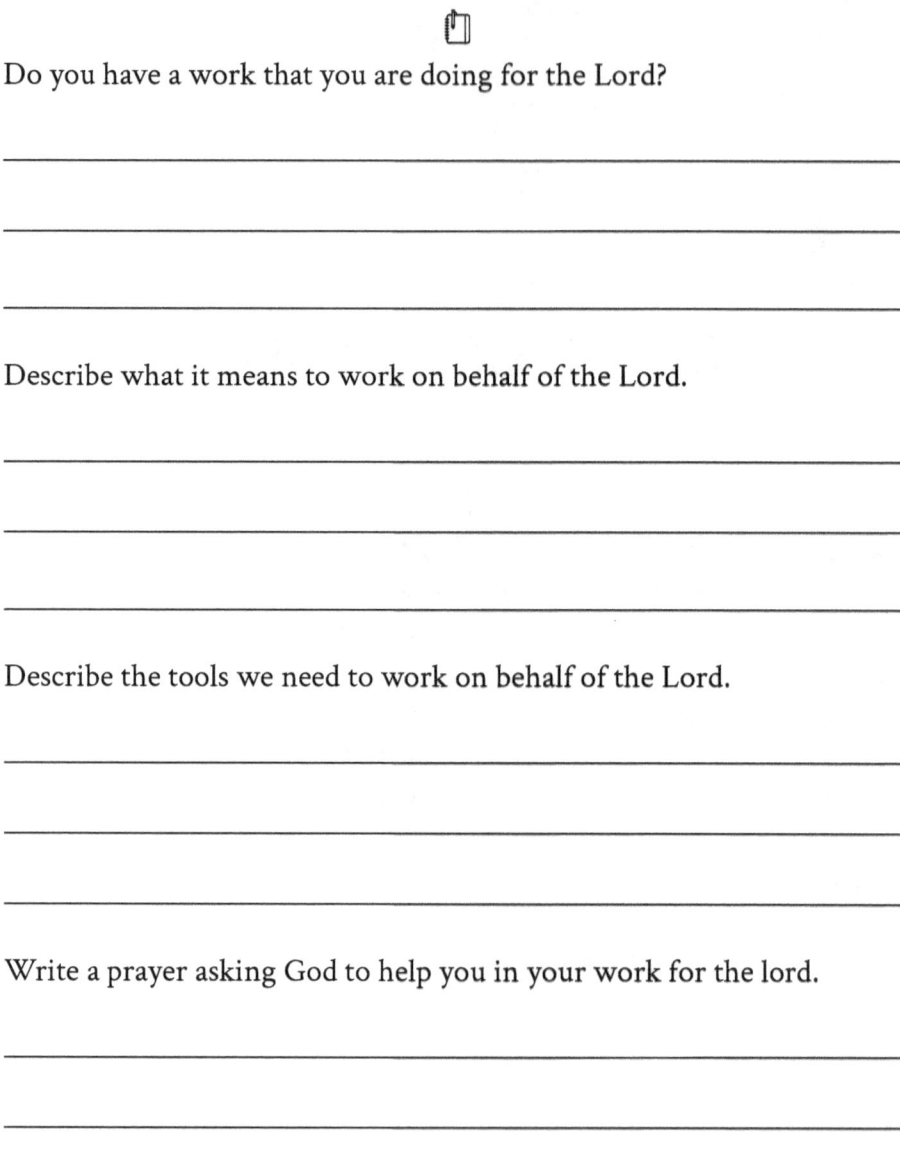

Do you have a work that you are doing for the Lord?

_____

_____

_____

Describe what it means to work on behalf of the Lord.

_____

_____

_____

Describe the tools we need to work on behalf of the Lord.

_____

_____

_____

Write a prayer asking God to help you in your work for the lord.

_____

_____

_____

_____

_____

_____

_____

_____

_____

_____

_____

_____

_____

"Jesus said to him, 'Thomas, because you have seen Me, you have believed. Blessed are those who have not seen and yet have believed'" And truly Jesus did many other signs in the presence of His disciples, which are not written in this book.
(JOHN 20:29-30, NKJV)

DAY 35
COMMUNE WITH GOD

My Lord. And my God.

We need to become aware of Your presence. It's all about seeing Your glory and the gifts that You give. We need to see You working in our community, through Your people, and working in our lives. Open our eyes that we may see Your great deeds. Remind us of the many blessings You have given us. Heighten our senses to Your presence. Teach us how to commune with You—for You are God with us.

We want to feel the comfort of Your love in a private moment. Overpower us with Your Holy Spirit so that we can bathe in Your glory. Then we will recognize Your soft, still voice, stop and smell the Rose of Sharon and the Lily of the Valleys. We will ignore the annoying chatter around us so we can tune into Your closeness and experience Your presence.

The power of Your presence will make us reach out and touch the hem of Your garment. Be a resident in our home and a constant reminder of Your shed blood for our sins. Then we will be able to commune with You.

To God be the glory forever and ever. Amen.

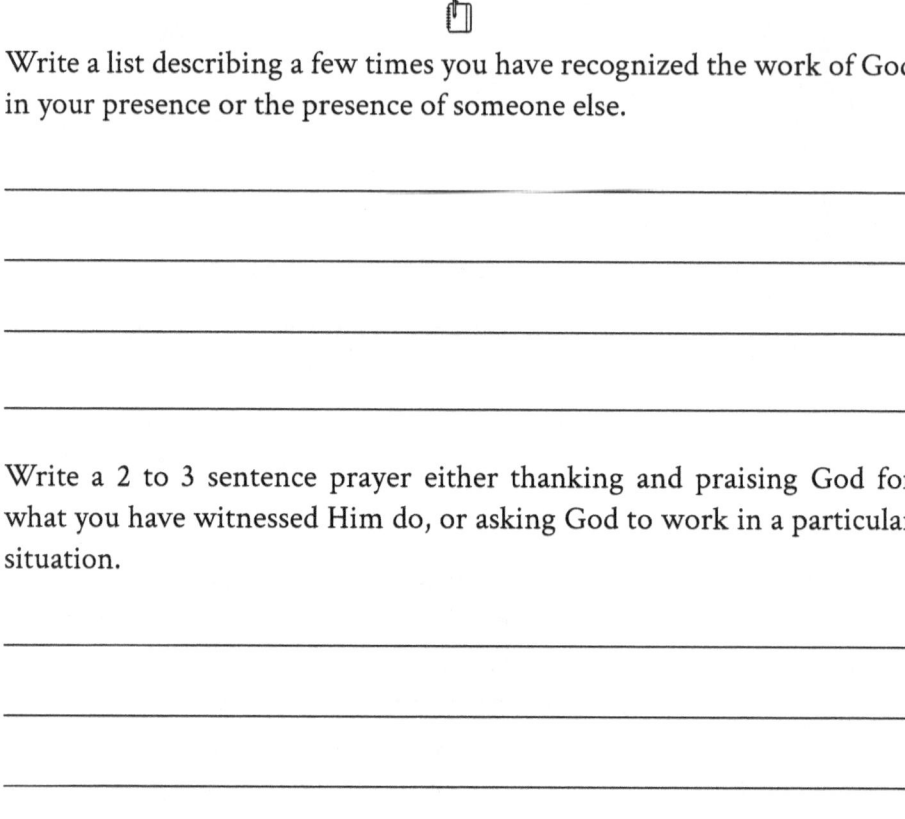

Write a list describing a few times you have recognized the work of God in your presence or the presence of someone else.

_____

_____

_____

_____

Write a 2 to 3 sentence prayer either thanking and praising God for what you have witnessed Him do, or asking God to work in a particular situation.

_____

_____

_____

_____

_____

_____

_____

_____

_____

_____

_____

_____

_____

_____

†

"But we all, with unveiled face, beholding as in a mirror the glory of the Lord, are being transformed into the same image from glory to glory, just as by the Spirit of the Lord."

(2 CORINTHIANS 3:18, NKJV)

DAY 36
POWERFUL COMBINATION OF TOOLS

Heavenly Father, since we have decided to follow Jesus our Lord, You have given us powerful combinations of tools to help transform our lives.

With the spirit of compassion and kind-heartedness, we can turn sadness into joy. With faith and hope, we can defeat pessimism and doubt. With patience and persistence, we can see the finished product of our hard work and prayers. With sacrifice and self-giving, we can show the love of God. With our dedication and sincerity, we can turn discouragement into optimism.

So we say thank You for the many tools You have given us to defend ourselves in spiritual warfare, so that we can live productive lives. We praise You for making us victors and not victims.

Because of You, we stand proud to be children of the Most High God. We are optimistic about our future and reject the message of doom. With these tools, we are being transformed into new creations for Christ—a better mother, a better father, a better friend, and a better neighbor. As a result, the world is a better place, because we have been transformed into better citizens of our communities.

With these combinations of tools, we are being transformed into the likeness of Your beloved Son, our Lord Jesus Christ. Now we are encouraged by our own experience of change—changed by the authoritative

Word of God. Now we rejoice that God has given us eyewitnesses of transformed lives. It is all because of You, O Lord. We shall forever look to You for help, for vision, and for inspiration.

This is my earnest prayer. Amen.

Through Christ Jesus God has given us a powerful combination of tools to help transform our lives. Have you utilized them all?

_____

_____

Which tools do you need to take out of the spiritual tool box and make good use of?

_____

_____

Why do you think as believers in Christ Jesus we neglect using them all?

_____

_____

How can we be reminded to do so?

_____

_____

_____

_____

_____

_____

_____

_____

_____

_____

_____

_____

"Let us draw near with a true heart in full assurance of faith, having our hearts sprinkled from an evil conscience and our bodies washed with pure water. Let us hold fast the confession of our hope without wavering, for He who promised is faithful."
(HEBREWS 10:22-23, NKJV)

DAY 37

ETERNAL ASSURANCE

Most Gracious God, give us eternal assurance. Inspire Your people to believe that he who looks through the eyes of faith—rather than doubt—is highly blessed. Help us to realize how fortunate the faithful are. They maintain awareness of the grace of God.

If they experience a shipwreck in their lives, they remember to be thankful for the lifeboat. They are like the person who falls down but simply gets up and keeps walking without complaining. Despite the many naysayers and those who have nothing positive to say, the faithful take on the attitude of Christ Jesus.

Aid our ability to see past our present situation and recognize the goodness coming our way. We don't want to miss the silver lining because of clouds of doubt. We want the ability to capture the wind, direct our sails, and be guided to the shores.

We are hoping for a bright future—not standing in place doing nothing, but working toward a better tomorrow. We want to see the glowing light shatter the darkness. Let our work of faith be defined by Eternal Assurance. For we labor with persistence through the Christian journey.

As a result, we will see our names written in the Lamb's Book of Life.

In the name of the Father, the Son, and the Holy Spirit, I pray. Amen.

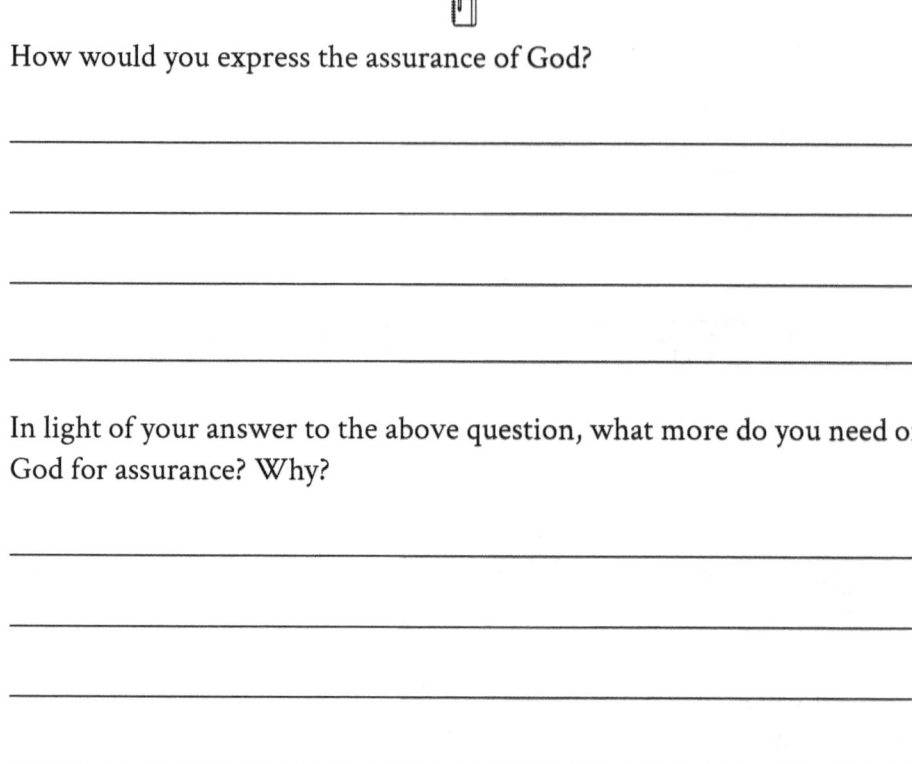

How would you express the assurance of God?

_____

_____

_____

_____

In light of your answer to the above question, what more do you need of God for assurance? Why?

_____

_____

_____

_____

_____

_____

_____

_____

_____

_____

_____

_____

_____

_____

†

"For I have no one like-minded, who
will sincerely care for your state.
For all seek their own, not the things
which are of Christ Jesus."
(PHILIPIANS 2:20-21, NKJV)

DAY 38
CONCERN ABOUT GOD

At first, it might sound strange that a mortal man can be concerned about the immortal God. But occasionally, we should ask the question: Have we not done anything to please Him? By doing so, we will have put our concerns on the back burner—just for a moment—and placed what concerns God on the front burner.

What can I do for You, O Lord? I am constantly asking for things from You; now I am asking—what can I do for You? For just a moment, I am not concerned for my health or safety, but I am concerned about whether You are pleased with me. Is there delight in Your heart for the work I have done? Are You satisfied with the way I live my life?

Have I learned how to touch Your heart? Have I learned how to use my faith in everyday life? These are my most important concerns. Help me understand that it is not hard to please You—I simply need to care about what You care about. I need to seek Your heart's desires. I need to be interested in how You feel.

I know that if I exercise my faith, it will be pleasing in Your sight. I pray that my concerns are in alignment with Your concerns. Thank You for being patient with my insensitivity and lack of compassion toward You.

Hear my prayer, dear Lord. Amen.

Is it hard for a person who has modest means or hardly any means, to care for and show compassion toward a person who seemingly has everything?

_____

_____

_____

_____

Explain the dynamics involved in this effort.

_____

_____

_____

_____

What gift would you give a person who seemingly has everything?

_____

_____

_____

_____

_____

_____

_____

_____

_____

_____

_____

_____

_____

"Ascribe strength to God; His excellence is over Israel, and His strength is in the clouds. O God, You are more awesome than Your holy places. The God of Israel is He who gives strength and power to His people. Blessed be God!"
(PSALM 68:34-35, NKJV)

DAY 39

BELIEVING IN THE UNLIMITED POWER OF GOD IN US

Lord, help us to believe in Your unlimited power. And help us to believe in the power within ourselves. Speak to us, Lord, so that we will know we are bigger than what we believe we are.

Increase our faith in You—and in ourselves. Help us to cast out all doubt. Let our imagination run wild, and help us believe in the power You gave us. Strengthen our belief in the power that can propel us to higher heights.

We don't know our limits until we've tried to reach them—and even then, You can break the limits and take us even further. Surprise us, Lord, with what You can do through us. Convince us that there is no limit to what You can do through those who believe in You.

As we allow You to use us, You will reveal that we are better than what we used to be. We can go further than we think we can. Help us to surrender our will to Yours so You can pull the best out of us. Help us to give ourselves away to You in all things.

I pray in Jesus' holy name. Amen.

What are some of the things that prevent or hinder us from believing what God can do through us?

_____

_____

_____

_____

List some ways that you believe that can help us overcome those things that prevent or hinder us from believing in the unlimited power of God working in our lives.

_____

_____

_____

_____

_____

_____

_____

_____

_____

_____

_____

_____

_____

_____

"My brethren, count it all joy when you fall into various trials, knowing that the testing of your faith produces patience. But let patience have its perfect work, that you may be perfect and complete, lacking nothing."
(JAMES 1:2-4, NKJV)

DAY 40

ENDURING PAIN

Heavenly Father, when times are difficult and heartbreaking, I need to remember that You are the One who strengthens me. Even in situations that are intimidating and dark, help me remember that You are always nearby. I know You are right beside me.

You have provided a soothing Spirit to come and mend my broken heart. Thank You for keeping me safe in Your hands and leading me through troubled times. I realize that life is a journey—fraught with both joyful and dark moments. The darkness of night makes the dawn of morning brighter.

I am thankful for the hope of tomorrow that You instill in me, and for the much-needed strength on life's journey when met with occasional pain—knowing that it will not always be the same. Thank You for encouraging me. There is joy in seeing the wonders of the Lord through it all.

How great is Your compassion that comforts me.

In Christ's name, I pray. Amen.

It is not easy to consider trials a joyful experience. Yet that is what we are encouraged to do. When we trust God and rely on Him, we can know we are being purified and made perfect.

Is there a trial you need to thank God for?

_____

_____

_____

_____

Have the Scriptures given you a way to endure your trials?

_____

_____

_____

_____

During your experience, how helpful is the process of seeking God's presence?

_____

_____

_____

_____

_____

_____

_____

_____

_____

_____

_____

_____

_____

www.ingramcontent.com/pod-product-compliance
Lightning Source LLC
Chambersburg PA
CBHW031525120626
46545CB00005B/2013